VEGETARIAN GRILLING

VEGETARIAN GRILLING

Karen Schulz // Maren Jahnke
With photographs by Wolfgang Kowall

60 Recipes for a Meatless Summer

Skyhorse Publishing

PREPARING VEGAN RECIPES

Some of the recipes in this book are vegan and are marked by a ⓥ. Many others can be made vegan by replacing a few ingredients.

VEGETARIAN	VEGAN
Butter	Vegan margarine
Milk	Soy milk
Cream	Soy cream
Yogurt	Soy yogurt
Cream cheese	Vegan cream cheese
Goat cheese	Vegan goat cheese
Feta cheese	Soy cheese
Honey	Maple syrup

Some wines or other alcoholic drinks are made with animal products such as gelatin, but vegan alternatives are often available. Check the ingredients with the manufacturers.

CONTENTS

ENJOYING THE OUTDOORS 8
GETTING STARTED 10

SKEWERED 19
WRAPPED AND ROLLED 40
GRILLED 60
STUFFED 82

DIPS AND SPICES 102
TO ROUND IT OFF 116

INDEX 134
THE TEAM 142

ENJOYING THE OUTDOORS

Vegetarian grilling? When we told our friends and family about our new book project, we received the most varied reactions—from compassionate, taunting laughter (from the men) to complete enthusiasm because the monotony of grilling was about to come to an end (from the women). The latter was really our inspiration for this book.

As recipe creators, we are fairly critical about the traditional, archaic style of preparing food over an open fire. No matter which garden, park, or beach one is invited in the summer or even during colder temperatures, the grill is always there. In the worst case scenario, that means consuming sausage or pork cutlets doused in store-bought sauce several times a week, or if you are a vegetarian, being content with a foil-baked potato or possibly a piece of dry, grilled Feta cheese. Too often, we find ourselves politely declining the offerings from the grill and instead resigning ourselves to the salads, breads, and dips (which should ideally only provide an attractive background for the main courses).

After experiencing such events, our enthusiasm for this truly beautiful form of collective cooking and eating was markedly dampened. And we asked ourselves whether anything could be done about this, other than a complete denial of grilling. Together, we began to dream of colorful vegetable skewers, delicately grilled vegetable chunks, and fragrantly painted fruits. Since it was clear from the moment we started brainstorming that we weren't interested in meat or fish, the idea was born—we would create vegetarian grilling recipes!

We were inspired by cooking styles from all over the world. We skewered, wrapped, and rolled up in our recipes much more than the typical selection from the grocery store or the cheese shop. Many meatless delights for the palate came to our "Test Grill," seasoned with spicy marinades or homemade spice mixtures. As we tinkered and sampled, we were convinced that we were not writing a "women's book." Even our male test eaters allowed the phrase, "Huh, almost better than meat!" to pass their lips while trying one or another dish—and then proceeded to devour it.

Of course, it is your decision whether your grill will be dedicated solely to vegetarian dishes or whether they will instead be featured side by side with an assortment of meats. In any case, we hope that our recipes provide some diversity and new culinary experiences to make your grill gatherings more colorful and enjoyable!

KAREN SCHULZ AND MAREN JAHNKE

GETTING STARTED

INGREDIENTS

QUALITY

In cooking, the results depend on the quality of the ingredients. In order that the effort is worth it and eating a pleasure, we try to buy organic produce. It almost always tastes better and richer, contains fewer pollutants, and puts less strain on the environment, which provides us with a clear conscience. It is, of course, best when one knows and trusts the farmer who grows the produce. Fruits and vegetables are at their highest quality when they are in season. The shorter travel times give them extra freshness and aroma, since they matured in the sunlight instead of in a greenhouse.

WHERE DO I BUY?

The fun of cooking can begin in your area while buying the ingredients at a well-stocked farmer's market, an organic produce store, a good retail store, or a health food store. While some ingredients for the recipes can be found in a deli, an organic store, or an Asian food store, most can be obtained in a good supermarket. And the Internet is becoming a better and better source, especially for rare foods and spices.

HOW DO I PREPARE?

When grilling, most of the preparation is moved from the kitchen out into the open—ideally, you should be able to enjoy the scenery while serenely turning the grill. Nevertheless, some work still must be done in the kitchen; vegetables, tofu, cheese, etc., have to be cleaned, cut, and possibly marinated or stuffed. Many ingredients can be prepared beforehand and stored in a refrigerator or a cooler. Do read the recipes well in advance so you will have a general idea of what needs to be done and to ward off stress and panic because you did not factor in the time for marinating, for example. Yeast mixtures for the breads may be prepared in advance and cooled; the same goes for the other preparatory steps. Potatoes, onions, etc., can be precooked a day in advance. But sauces, marinades, and spice mixtures can be prepared days or even weeks in advance and stored in a closed, secure space. Add dressing to salads with delicate greens right before serving so they do not become soggy.

MARINATING – HOW LONG?

The times given in our marinade recipes refer to minimum marinating times. Soy products, cheeses, and robust vegetables and fruits that do not change color after being cut will not suffer from a longer marinade than stated—in fact, the taste will often improve. This can turn the preparation into an even more relaxed process since you can begin it earlier. If some of the ingredients in a marinade recipe give you pause (for example, if you are cautious about chili peppers or garlic), you can use shorter marinating times or add these ingredients later.

VEGETABLES ON THE GRILL: WHAT'S DIFFERENT?

Vegetarian ingredients almost always contain less fat. This is very important to know when preparing them on the grill, since the vegetable ingredients may dry out or even burn if they are not marinated or brushed with olive oil or another vegetable oil. Even seitan and tofu, whether pure, cured, or in sausage form, should be watched closely while grilling. Both consist mainly of protein, which means you need a little know-how and patience to grill them correctly to crispiness. The best thing to do is to start with one or two recipes with these ingredients and combine them with uncomplicated vegetable variations. And be heavy on the brush when cooking protein-heavy foods so that they do not dry out.

PLANNING

GROUPS

It is difficult to give advice for planning a barbecue or a party with many guests. Not even hosts who know the guests can say for certain how hungry they will be on the big day, but it is good to keep in mind that men generally eat more grilled food than women, who prefer salads and appetizers.

In planning a barbecue, be sure to offer several dishes from this book—even men find a vegetable skewer, stuffed portabella mushrooms, or a grilled panini beguiling and will choose to partake. Factor in a number of recipes with filling, nourishing ingredients containing cheese or soy products, potatoes, or bread. Each guest should be served at least one portion, and preferably one to two additional portions heavy on vegetables or fruit. In addition, have sufficient dips and salads containing satisfying ingredients such as noodles, lentils, and beans to fill out even light vegetable dishes perfectly. And, of course, don't forget the bread—whether it's cooked on the grill or bought from a store.

SETUP

Always set up your grill with enough distance from your neighbors and house so no one is disturbed. Make sure your grill is secure, and place a small table within reach for utensils, raw ingredients, and prepared food. For practicality's sake, set out a stack of plates or platters for transporting dishes to and from the table. Have sufficient dishes to sample because they will be snatched up right away by guests and will not need to be sent back. If you are working with fire, set up some fire safety equipment nearby, such as a fire blanket, a bucket of sand, or a fire extinguisher. Lay out oven gloves or large potholders by the table so that no one burns their fingers, and make sure you have burn gel in a nearby refrigerator or cooler to offer quick relief in case of a burn.

GRILLING

PREHEATING

Even with a coal grill, it is almost inevitable that the coals are never at the right temperature, a grilling paradox. In our experience, one can't argue with grilling masters, but our advice is to heat up the grill in advance so that the coals are no longer burning when you begin in earnest. Of course, correct preheating is also important with other grilling equipment.

COOKING TIME

Many grill masters swear by their equipment. Naturally, there are significant differences between classic coal grills, gas or electric grills, and oven grills. While one can usually tell the temperature of an oven grill exactly, the coal grill simply gets "pretty hot." Different temperatures can also be achieved by varying the distance of the grate from the heat source, the method of grilling (do you turn the food over often, or do you let it sizzle?), and the desired level of crispiness, so the cooking times in the recipes are really just guidelines. When cooking vegetables, the danger of undercooking is diminished taste rather than health hazards, but if something needs a shorter or longer time to cook, we still urge you to trust your own experience and instinct before the time in the recipe.

UTENSILS

Traditional kitchen utensils are not entirely sufficient when cooking outdoors; a few additional pieces are necessary or just practical.

COOKING BRUSHES

Cooking brushes are indispensable for distributing oil and marinade evenly. When choosing a brush, consider its resistance to heat—a brush should not scorch at higher temperatures. Classic brushes are made with boar bristles. Make sure to choose a high-quality brush so that the bristles will not fall out and stick to the food. Silicone brushes are resilient and dishwasher-friendly. Our tip for extra fragrance—make a brush out of herbs. Hardy herbs such as rosemary, thyme, or lavender tied together with kitchen yarn are best and can be used with oils and marinades (see page 11).

SKEWERS

We recommend investing in metal skewers, which have several advantages. They are reusable indefinitely, conduct the heat from the grill into the interior of the skewered food, help the food cook from the inside out, and will not burn you even when left at a short distance from the heat. If you only have wood or bamboo skewers available, soak them in water beforehand or cover them with oil while brushing the food to reduce the risk of them burning during cooking. For a more refined option, use skewers that add flavor by spearing the food on thick rosemary or lemongrass stalks. Rotation is something of a gauntlet because the pieces may refuse to rotate as you turn the skewer. You may wish to use two skewers in parallel or even obtain double skewers designed for this reason (see page 38—Pimento Skewers).

GRILLING TONGS

Tongs are possibly the most important utensil you will use. Only they can ensure that your fingers remain unburned even in the vicinity of high temperatures. It is very important that they have a secure grip, like oversized pincers. Choose the length based on the size of the grill—small kitchen tongs will not work well with a large outdoor grill, and you will end up burning yourself. We especially like the handmade wooden tongs from the German company, Oz-Goods (www.oz-goods.de) because they lie in your hand like worry stones and let you grasp with precision.

ALUMINUM BAKING PANS

If the grilled food is finely cut or very soft, or if the marinade drips copiously, you should not let the food cook directly over the coals since the bits that drip or fall through will burn up and leave unhealthy residue on the grill. In this case, it is better to use an aluminum baking pan that sits on the grate. This method requires some patience since it prolongs the grilling process because heat no longer reaches the food directly. We recommend selecting recipes where not all of the food requires a pan so that the first delicacies coming off the grill can satisfy the most immediate hunger.

GRILL BASKETS

Practical grill baskets used for fish can be very helpful in vegetarian grilling, especially when grilling whole cobs of corn or other larger pieces such as whole leeks, tomatoes, or halved peppers. When these are securely fastened in a grill basket, they will not slip through the grate and will receive the full blast of the heat.

YIELDS 4 SKEWERS

5 tsp (15 g) pine nuts
1 shallot
About 3 sprigs of sage
½ cup (125 g) cream cheese
24 medium portobello
mushrooms, about 12 oz (350 g)
Olive oil for brushing
Salt and freshly ground
black pepper

4 metal skewers
Aluminum baking sheet

Roast the pine nuts in a nonoiled pan, cool on a plate, and then chop coarsely. Peel and chop the shallots. Wash the sage sprigs, dabbing the leaves dry, and setting a few large leaves off to the side. Finely chop the remaining leaves and mix with cream cheese, shallots, and pine nuts. Spice thoroughly with salt and pepper.

Clean the mushrooms and remove stems. Fill the mushroom caps with about a tablespoon of cream cheese. Slide about six mushrooms onto each skewer, placing them in pairs with the filled sides pressing together and separated by the remaining sage leaves.

Brush the skewers with oil and grill on a baking sheet over a hot grill for eight to ten minutes, rotating.

> **TIP** Goes well with the Rosemary Flatbread (page 126) or the String Bean and Couscous Salad (page 119).

Wash the potatoes thoroughly and boil for fifteen to twenty minutes. Rinse with cold water and let the potatoes dry a little. Wash the rosemary sprigs, dabbing them dry and removing the lower needles.

Peel the garlic and chop finely with the rosemary needles. Stir together with oil, salt, and pepper. Carefully push the rosemary sprigs through the potatoes. Brush with the rosemary oil mixture and grill over high heat for five minutes while rotating and brushing with the oil. Salt to taste.

TIP Goes well with the Olive-Almond Tapenade (page 115).

1 lb (500 g) small, young potatoes
4 long, strong sprigs of rosemary, about 10 in (25 cm)
1 clove of garlic
4 tbsp olive oil
Sea salt and freshly ground black pepper

YIELDS 6 SKEWERS

2–3 tsp (5½ g) Lemongrass
Gomashio (page 104)
4 tbsp teriyaki marinade
5 tbsp vegetable oil
9 oz (250 g) firm tofu
1½ cup (100 g) shiitake mushrooms
12 jarred baby corn
cobs, about 3.5 oz (100g)
12 Makrut lime leaves

6 metal skewers

Mix the Gomashio with the teriyaki marinade and oil. Dry tofu and cut into twelve cubes. Place the tofu in the marinade, refrigerate, and leave to soak for at least two hours.

Wash the mushrooms. Dry the baby corn. Remove the tofu from the marinade and set the marinade aside. Place tofu cubes on the skewers, alternating with the mushrooms, Makrut lime leaves, and baby corn. Grill over high heat for about six minutes, turning often, and brushing with the marinade.

> **TIP** Goes well with the Glass Noodle Salad (page 122). You can find the teriyaki marinade and the Makrut lime leaves in an Asian grocery store.

24

CITRUS ZUCCHINI-
FETA SKEWERS

YIELDS 4 SKEWERS

Cut Feta into large cubes. Crush the peppercorns. Wash lemons with hot water. Grate the peel of half a lemon and squeeze the juice from that half. Mix the olive oil, lemon juice, and lemon peel with the crushed peppercorns and add a little salt. Place the Feta cubes in the mixture and let them sit for at least thirty minutes.

Wash the zucchini, pat them dry, and cut or shave lengthwise into thin sections. Chop the remaining half of the lemon. Remove the Feta cubes from the oil and wrap a zucchini section around each cube. Set about three pieces on each skewer and top each skewer with a piece of lemon.

Grill over high heat for eight to ten minutes while brushing with the remaining citrus-and-pepper oil.

2 cup (200 g) Feta cheese
1 tsp pink peppercorns
1 lemon
2 tbsp olive oil
2 zucchini, about 7 oz (200 g)
Salt

4 metal skewers

TIP Goes well with Mint Yogurt (page 112) or the Colorful Sun Rolls (page 129).

CAPRESE SKEWERS

1 large bundle of basil
1 tsp anise seeds
6 tbsp olive oil
1 clove of garlic
1½ cup (250 g) small yellow and
red cherry tomatoes
1 cup (150 g) mini mozzarella balls,
about 20
Salt and freshly ground black
peppercorn

6 metal skewers
Aluminum baking pan

Wash the basil, shake it dry in a colander, and remove the leaves. Set aside a third of the larger leaves and finely chop the rest. Grind the anise seeds finely in a mortar and mix them with the chopped basil and olive oil. Peel the garlic and press it into the oil. Add salt and pepper.

Wash the tomatoes. Dry the mozzarella pieces. Alternate whole tomatoes and mozzarella pieces on the skewers with the remaining basil leaves, folded.

Brush the skewers with the basil oil and grill over a baking pan for five minutes, rotating and brushing with basil oil until the cheese is soft but not melted.

TIP Goes well with the Noodle and Lentil Salad (page 123).

28

PROVENCE SKEWERS

Wash the eggplant and cut lengthwise into fourths and then into thin sections. Peel the shallots, halving the larger ones. Wash and halve the tomatoes. Dry the artichoke hearts and cut into fourths.

Peel the garlic and chop finely. Mix with olive oil, spices, salt, and pepper. Alternate on the skewer the eggplant slices, tomatoes, shallots, and artichokes.

Brush the skewers with spiced oil and grill for eight to ten minutes over high heat while rotating. Keep brushing with the remaining oil.

TIP Goes well with the String Bean and Couscous Salad (page 119).

1 eggplant, about 9 oz (250 g)
8 shallots, about 5 oz (150g)
14 oz (400 g) small, firm tomatoes
4 pickled artichoke hearts
1–2 cloves of garlic
7 tbsp (100 ml) olive oil
1 tsp Herbs de Provence
Salt and freshly ground black peppercorn

8 metal skewers

29

6 METAL SKEWERS

2 corn cobs
1 red bell pepper
2 red onions
1 firm, ripe avocado
1–2 tbsp olive oil for brushing
5 tbsp (65 g) Coriander-Chili Butter
(page 112)
Salt

Peel the leaves from the corn cobs and remove the silk. Boil the corn in salt water for about forty minutes. Rinse, let it cool, and cut into thin sections.

Wash and halve the bell pepper, removing the seeds and cutting into large pieces. Peel the onions and cut into thin sections. Cut the avocado into fourths, remove the pit, then peel, and cut into pieces. Place the avocado on the skewers, alternating with red bell pepper, corn, and onion.

Grill over high heat for ten to fifteen minutes, turning regularly and brushing with oil. Remove the skewers, place them on a platter, and top them off with coriander-chili butter.

TIP Serve with some taco chips. To save cooking time, you can also use pre-cooked corn cobs for the skewers.

30

FLATBREAD SKEWERS

Wash the tomatoes and cut into segments. Dry peppers, halving larger ones. Cut the flatbread and cheese into about twelve cubes each. Spear the tomatoes, peppers, bread, and cheese onto the skewers, alternating.

Mix the olive oil with the oregano and sumac. Add salt and pepper. Drizzle the oil over the skewers and let it soak in for about fifteen minutes. Grill the skewers over high heat for about eight minutes, brushing with spiced oil.

TIP Sumac is a dark red, sour spice used in Arabian cuisine and can be found in Turkish grocery stores.

2 tomatoes

8 pickled mild chili peppers

4 oz Turkish flatbread

7 oz (200 g) firm sheep cheese

5 tbsp olive oil

1 tsp dried oregano

1 tsp sumac

Salt and freshly ground black peppercorn

6 metal skewers

COLORFUL
SOY SAUSAGE SKEWERS

YIELDS 6 SKEWERS

1 oz white onions, jarred

1 yellow bell pepper

1 cup (150 g) cherry tomatoes

7 oz smoked soy sausage

2 tbsp tomato ketchup

1 tsp curry powder

1 tbsp vegetable oil

2 tbsp orange juice

Salt and freshly ground black
pepper

6 metal skewers

Drain the onions and let them dry. Wash and halve the bell pepper, removing seeds and chopping into pieces. Wash tomatoes and pat dry. Cut the soy sausage into narrow pieces. Mix the ketchup, curry powder, oil, orange juice, salt, and pepper.

Place onions, peppers, tomatoes, and sausage on skewers, alternating. Brush with curry ketchup and grill over high heat for ten minutes, rotating.

TIP Other vegetarian proteins such as tofu or seitan may be substituted in this recipe.

HALLOUMI AND APRICOT SKEWERS

YIELDS 4–5 SKEWERS

9 oz (250 g) Halloumi cheese
3 scallions
4 apricots
About 10 fresh laurel leaves
2 tbsp vegetable oil
1 tsp Pepper Spice Mix (page 104)
Salt

4–5 metal skewers

Rinse the Halloumi under running water, pat dry, and cut into equal-sized cubes. Wash the scallions and chop them into pieces. Wash the apricots, pat dry, and cut into fourths, removing pits.

Place Halloumi cubes, laurel leaves, scallions, and apricot pieces on the skewers, alternating. Mix the oil with the Pepper Spice Mix. Brush the oil over the skewers and leave the skewers to marinate until ready to grill. Grill over high heat for about ten minutes while brushing with the remaining oil. Salt to taste.

TIP You may substitute firm sheep cheese or Feta for the Halloumi. Canned apricots may also be used instead of fresh fruit.

PIMIENTO SKEWERS

YIELDS 4 SKEWERS

32 Pimientos de Padrón
(mild, dark green peppers)
about 10 oz (300 g)
4 tbsp (60 ml) Chili-Mint Oil
(page 107)
Fleur de sel

4–8 metal skewers

Wash and drain the pimientos, placing about eight on each skewer. Grill for about five to seven minutes, brushing with Chili-Mint Oil.

Place the skewers on a platter, drizzle with the remaining oil and a little Fleur de sel.

TIP The skewers are easier to rotate if you use two skewers or a double skewer. Then the Pimientos cannot turn back around on themselves.

WRAPPED
AND ROLLED

HALLOUMI ENVELOPES WITH FRUIT SALSA

YIELDS 4 ENVELOPES

9 oz (250 g) Halloumi cheese
4 servings Fruit Salsa (page 108)
about 4 tsp olive oil for brushing
½ tsp Pepper Spice Mix (page 104)

Aluminum foil

Rinse the cheese well under cold water, dab dry, and cut it into cubes.
Mix with Fruit Salsa.

Cut four squares of foil and brush each lightly with oil. Divide the Halloumi-salsa mixture between the squares. Drizzle each with about one teaspoon of olive oil and some Pepper Spice Mix. Close the foil envelopes and grill over high heat for eight to ten minutes.

TIP Halloumi can be very salty, so try a piece in advance and rinse it thoroughly, if needed.

43

BARBECUE WRAP WITH VEGETABLES

YIELDS 4 SERVINGS

1 sweet potato, about 10 oz (300 g)

2 green bell peppers

8 scallions

1 romaine lettuce heart

Sunflower oil for brushing

4 wraps, about 1½ oz each

4 tbsp Barbecue Sauce
with Apricots (page 111)

Salt and freshly ground black
pepper

Aluminum baking pan

Peel the sweet potato and shave into very thin slices. Wash and halve the bell peppers, removing the seeds and cutting into strips. Clean scallions and cut into pieces. Clean romaine lettuce heart and cut into fourths, but do not remove the stalk.

Place the sweet potato and pepper pieces on a baking pan, brush them with some oil, and grill for about eight minutes, rotating the pieces. Brush the lettuce and scallions, and grill for the last one to two minutes of grilling. Salt and pepper lightly.

Heat the wraps directly on the grill for thirty to sixty seconds until they are flexible. Brush with about one tablespoon of Barbecue Sauce, add the vegetables, and roll the wraps up.

> **TIP** Serve the wraps with additional Barbecue Sauce for dipping.

EGGPLANT ENVELOPES WITH SMOKED TOFU

Drain the tomatoes. Cut the tofu into ten pieces and brush with Ajvar. Wash the eggplant, rub dry, and cut lengthwise into ten thin slices. Brush the eggplant slices with oil on both sides and salt and pepper. Grill the slices for about six to ten minutes over high heat.

Remove the eggplant slices from the grill and lay about one piece of tofu and one tomato on top of each. Roll up and secure with metal skewers. Grill the envelopes for about five minutes, rotating.

TIP Serve the Eggplant Envelopes over baby spinach.

10 sun-dried tomatoes in oil, about ¾ cup (80 g)

9 oz (250 g) smoked tofu

2 tbsp Ajvar (pepper mousse, jarred)

1 large eggplant, about 18 oz

3 tbsp oil

Salt and freshly ground black peppercorn

10 small metal skewers

47

SWEET CRÊPES WITH GRILLED PEACHES

5 tbsp butter

2 medium eggs

4 tbsp (30 g) powdered sugar

13 tbsp (100 g) flour

½ cup (300 ml) milk

½ cup (120 g) crème fraîche

1 packet bourbon vanilla sugar

1–2 tbsp Marsala wine

2 peaches

Melt three tablespoons of butter for the crème fraîche dough. Beat the eggs and powdered sugar with an egg whisk. Mix in the flour and milk and let the mixture sit for thirty minutes. Mix in the melted butter. Melt about one-half tablespoon of butter in a pan, pour in about a fourth of the mixture, and bake into a thin, golden-yellow crêpe.

Mix the crème fraîche together with vanilla sugar and Marsala. Wash and dry the peaches, and remove pits. Grill the peach halves over high heat for about four minutes, rotating. Place the vanilla cream on the insides of the peaches. Lay out each peach half, fold it into a crêpe, and grill for an additional two minutes on each side.

TIP Try using nougat or hazelnut cream instead of vanilla cream.

48

SWISS CHARD AND TOFU ENVELOPES

1 stalk of lemongrass
5 oz (150 ml) coconut milk
1 tbsp fish sauce or soy sauce
1 tsp green curry paste
9 oz (250 g) tofu
2 oz (50 g) bean sprouts
6 large leaves of swiss chard,
about 2 oz each (60 g)
Vegetable oil for brushing

6 small metal skewers

Remove the hard outer leaves from the lemongrass and chop them coarsely. Combine coconut milk, fish sauce, curry paste, and lemongrass in a pot and bring to a boil. Simmer over low heat for about ten minutes. Remove the lemongrass.

Drain the tofu and cut into six pieces. Mix the tofu with the curry-coconut cream, cover, and let marinate for at least thirty minutes. Wash the swiss chard under hot water and drain thoroughly. Wash the bean sprouts well, pat them dry, and cut off the hard stalk.

Place each piece of marinated tofu on a swiss chard leaf with some curry sauce and bean sprouts. Roll the leaves up and pierce them with skewers. Brush with a little oil and grill over high heat for about ten minutes.

> **TIP** You should be able to find fish sauce and curry paste in an Asian grocery or in a well-stocked supermarket.

NAPPA CABBAGE ENVELOPES WITH SPELT GRAIN FILLING

Clean the leeks and cut into narrow rings. Peel the shallot and chop finely. Heat up two tablespoons of oil in a pot. Cook the leeks and shallot in the oil. Add spelt grain and cook briefly, stirring. Pour in the vegetable broth, cover, and cook over low heat for about ten minutes to let the grain soften, stirring occasionally.

Wash the cabbage leaves and chop the hard core at a shallow angle. Blanch the cabbage leaves in boiling salted water for about one minute, drain and rinse with cold water, and place on a kitchen towel to dry.

Wash the apple and then cut it into fourths, removing the core. Cut the apple into small cubes, add to the pot, and cook briefly. Add curry, salt, and pepper. Place the filling in the cabbage leaves. Close the leaves shut around the filling, roll up, and secure with skewers. Brush with remaining oil and grill over high heat for about five minutes.

4 oz (100 g) leeks

1 shallot

4 tbsp olive oil

4 oz (100 g) spelt grain

1¾ cups (400 ml) vegetable broth

6 large nappa cabbage leaves, about 2 oz each (50 g)

4 oz (100 g) apples

1 tsp curry powder

Salt and freshly ground black pepper

6 small metal skewers

TIP Goes well with the Mint Yogurt (page 112). You can find spelt grain in organic food stores or health food stores.

STUFFED DATES IN PHYLLO DOUGH

12 large fresh dates,
about 11 oz (300 g)
1 oz (25 g) shelled walnuts
4 oz (100 g) creamy sheep cheese
7 tbsp (50 g) cream cheese
½ tsp Garam Masala
1 pinch cinnamon
2 oz (50 g) phyllo dough
Sunflower oil for brushing
Salt
Freshly ground black pepper

Wash the dates and pat dry. Cut lengthwise into the dates and remove the pits. Chop the walnuts. Mix sheep's cheese and cream cheese. Add walnuts and season with Garam Masala, cinnamon, salt, and pepper. Fill the dates with the mixture.

Spread the phyllo dough leaves out, side by side, on a damp kitchen towel. Brush the dough with oil and cut into twelve squares, about 3.5 x 10 in (9 x 15 cm). Roll each date in a dough square and brush with oil.

Grill the dates over high heat for three to four minutes, rotating until crispy.

TIP Goes well with Apple-Mango Chutney (page 113).

GRATINATED POTATOES

YIELDS 4 ENVELOPES

Thoroughly wash the potatoes and boil in water for about twenty-five minutes until soft. Drain, rinse with cold water, pat dry, and let cool.

Wash scallions and cut into thin rings. Wash the bell pepper and cut in half, removing the seeds and chopping into small cubes. Drain the corn. Finely grate the gouda and mix with sour cream. Spice strongly with cayenne pepper and a small amount of salt. Mix with leeks, corn, and pepper.

Halve the potatoes lengthwise and place cut side up on four oiled pieces of foil. Divide the vegetable and cheese mixture between the potatoes and close the pieces of foil into envelopes. Grill over high heat for about ten minutes.

> **TIP** The foil envelopes with potatoes and cream may be refrigerated for several hours prior to grilling.

4 potatoes, about 5 oz each (150 g)
7 scallions
½ red bell pepper
⅓ cup (50 g) canned corn
4 oz (120 g) Gouda
6 tbsp (80 g) sour cream
Oil for brushing
Salt and cayenne pepper

Aluminum foil

55

FENNEL AND APPLE ENVELOPES WITH GORGONZOLA

2 large fennel bulbs, about 14 oz each (400 g)

2 sour apples

2 tbsp fennel seeds

Zest of ½ lemon

6 tbsp olive oil, and some reserved for brushing

7 oz (200 g) Gorgonzola

Salt and freshly ground black pepper

Aluminum foil

Wash the fennel and remove the leaves, laying them to the side. Wash the bulbs, halve, remove the stem, and cut the fennel crosswise into thin sections. Wash the apples, cut into fourths, and then into thin sections.

Crush the fennel seeds in a mortar. Finely chop the green fennel leaves. Mix both with lemon zest, oil, and some salt and pepper. Mix with fennel and apple.

Form the aluminum foil into four envelopes, 8 x 8 in (20 x 20 cm), with shallow edges. Brush with oil in the middle and add fennel mixture. Cut the gorgonzola into cubes and divide it between the envelopes. Grill the open envelopes for eight to ten minutes.

TIP Goes well with Rosemary Flatbread (page 127).

56

GOAT CHEESE-STUFFED GRAPE LEAVES

8 large grape leaves in brine
2 sprigs of peppermint
5 oz (150 g) creamy goat cheese
1 tbsp chopped pistachios
About ½ tbsp ground cumin
Oil for brushing

Rinse the grape leaves thoroughly in a colander and drain dry.

Pick the mint leaves and chop finely. Mix the mint with the goat cheese and pistachios and spice with cumin.

Pat the grape leaves dry, removing the stems, if necessary. Place one to two tablespoons of cream onto each leaf. Fold the leaves and roll up securely. Brush the rolls lightly with oil all around and grill over high heat for about three minutes, rotating.

> **TIP** Some grape leaves in brine are extremely salty. It is a good idea to try a small piece ahead of time and soak the leaves for a few hours in cold water, if necessary.

GRILLED

MANGOES WITH SCALLION VINAIGRETTE

2 scallions
3 tsp wild honey
3 tbsp lemon juice
5 tbsp sunflower oil
4 ripe, firm mangoes
Salt and freshly ground black
pepper

Wash the scallions and chop finely. Mix the honey with lemon juice, salt, and pepper. Mix in the oil. Fold in the chopped scallions.

Cut two thick sections from the sides of the mangoes. Cut crosswise into the flesh of the mangoes, but do not cut through the skin. Brush the sections lightly with the scallion vinaigrette. Grill the mango halves face down for three minutes over high heat. Turn the pieces over and grill for an additional two minutes while brushing the mangoes with the remaining vinaigrette.

TIP Goes well with the Pimiento Skewers (page 38).

CORN COBS WITH CORIANDER-CHILI BUTTER

YIELDS 4 SERVINGS

Remove the leaves and silk from the corn cobs. Boil in water for thirty to forty minutes. Drain and rinse thoroughly.

Grill the corn over high heat for about fifteen minutes while brushing with four tablespoons of the Coriander-Chili Butter. Salt to taste. Put the remaining butter on the hot grilled corn.

TIP Goes well with the Fruit Salsa (page 108) and the canned jalapenos.

4 corn cobs
6 tbsp (80 g) Coriander-Chili Butter (page 112)
Salt

SOY PATTIES WITH OLIVES

YIELDS 4 SERVINGS

2½ oz (75 g) soy sausage
1½ oz green olives stuffed with
peppers
4–6 sprigs of thyme
2 large eggs
3 tbsp bread crumbs
2 tbsp olive oil
Salt and freshly ground black
pepper

Pour one cup (200 ml) of water over the sausages and soak. Meanwhile, chop the olives. Wash the thyme sprigs, shake them dry, remove the leaves from the stems, and chop finely. Mix the olives, thyme, eggs, and bread crumbs into the soy sausage with salt and pepper.

With damp hands, form the sausage mixture into four flat patties, brush with oil, and grill over high heat for about five minutes, turning the patties over while grilling.

TIP Goes well with Mint Yogurt (page 112). You can find soy sausage in organic food stores, health food stores, or well-stocked supermarkets.

66

ZUCCHINI WITH SUNFLOWER SEED PESTO

YIELDS 4 SERVINGS

Peel and chop the onion. Roast the sunflower seeds in an unoiled pan until golden-brown. Remove the seeds from the pan, and heat one tablespoon of olive oil and cook the onion.

Grate the Parmesan. Wash the basil and pat it dry. Remove the leaves from the stems and chop finely. Puree everything with the remaining oil, not too finely. Add salt and pepper to the pesto.

Wash the zucchini and pat dry. Cut diagonally across, but not all the way through the zucchini. Place the pesto in the diagonal cuts. Roll each zucchini in a piece of oiled foil and grill over high heat for about twenty minutes. Salt and pepper to taste.

1 onion
7 tbsp (60 g) sunflower seeds
8 tbsp olive oil
1½ oz (40 g) Parmesan cheese
1 bunch of basil
4 zucchini, about 9 oz each
Olive oil for brushing
Salt and freshly ground black pepper

Aluminum foil

TIP Goes well with the Wild Herb Salad with Tomatoes (page 125).

GRILLED ASPARAGUS
WITH GOAT CHEESE

1 bunch green asparagus, about
18 oz (500 g)
2 oz (50 g) goat cheese
5 tbsp (75 ml) Tarragon Oil
(page 107)
Salt to taste

Aluminum baking pan

Wash the asparagus and cut into thirds, removing the hard ends.
Crumble the goat cheese.

Brush the asparagus with Tarragon Oil and grill in a baking pan for about
ten minutes, rotating and continually brushing with oil. Place on a platter, drizzle
with remaining oil, and salt lightly to taste. Add the crumbled cheese on top.

TIP You can also grill the asparagus directly over the grill—just
make sure the oil does not drip.

SPICY EGGPLANTS

YIELDS 4 SERVINGS

2 large eggplants
4 tbsp Chili-Mint Oil (page 107)
Salt to taste

Wash the eggplants and halve them lengthwise, but do not remove the ends. Cut multiple times into the eggplant halves up to the stem and fan the pieces out.

Brush the eggplant halves with some Chili-Mint Oil and grill over high heat for about five minutes on each side. Keep brushing with the Chili-Mint Oil. Salt to taste.

TIP Goes well with the Colorful Sun Rolls (page 129).

73

GRILLED PINEAPPLE WITH VANILLA-GINGER SYRUP

¾ oz (20 g) ginger
1 tbsp butter
3½ tbsp brown sugar
juice of one lime
1 vanilla pod
2 tbsp chopped pistachios
1–2 tbsp dark rum to taste
1 pineapple

Peel the ginger and chop finely. Melt butter in a small pot. Add the ginger and cook for a short time. Add sugar and caramelize. Mix water with lemon juice until it yields 3½ tablespoons. Mix the juice into the caramelized ginger and bring to a boil.

Cut the vanilla pod open lengthwise and remove the beans. Add the vanilla pod and vanilla beans to the ginger stock and simmer for about ten minutes. Let cool. Remove the vanilla pod, mix in pistachios, and add rum to taste.

Peel the pineapple and cut into six thick sections. Grill the sections on each side for about three minutes over a hot grill, brushing with the vanilla-ginger syrup. Place the pineapple sections on a plate and drizzle with the remaining syrup.

TIP Goes well with homemade vanilla sauce or vanilla yogurt.

KURI SQUASH WITH MAPLE SYRUP AND WALNUT MARINADE

YIELDS 4 SERVINGS

26 oz (760 g) red kuri squash
A few leaves of romaine lettuce for serving
7 tbsp Maple Syrup and Walnut Marinade (page 108)
Salt

Wash squash, and then remove the seeds and fibrous core. Cut the squash into thin slices. Wash and drain the lettuce leaves and place them on a plate.

Brush the squash slices with the Maple Syrup and Walnut Marinade and grill over high heat for about ten minutes, rotating. Keep brushing with the marinade. Serve the squash on top of the lettuce leaves. Drizzle over with the remaining marinade and salt to taste.

> **TIP** If you use an aluminum baking pan, the squash will not get as dark, but you will have to double the cooking time.

77

MOZZARELLA WITH PERSIMMON-TOMATO CARPACCIO

1 bunch of flat leaf parsley

1 oz (30 g) gherkins, jarred

3 tsp capers, jarred

4 tbsp olive oil

2 beef tomatoes, about 18 oz (500 g)

1 large persimmon, about 11 oz (300 g)

2 balls of buffalo mozzarella, 4½ oz each (125 g)

Sea salt and freshly ground black pepper

Aluminum baking pan

Wash the parsley and shake it dry. Remove the leaves from stems and chop them. Drain the gherkins and capers, keeping two tablespoons of pickle water. Finely chop the gherkins and capers. Mix the pickle water with two tablespoons of oil and stir in gherkins, capers, and parsley. Add salt and pepper to parsley salsa.

Wash the tomatoes and the persimmon, and cut each into thin sections. Place the sections on the pan so that they overlap. Drain the mozzarella balls and halve and divide them among the sections. Drizzle over with remaining olive oil. Salt and pepper lightly.

Grill over high heat for about fifteen minutes until the cheese begins to melt, but still holds its form. Top the dish with parsley salsa and serve right away.

TIP Goes well with the Grilled Bread with Cheese and Onions (page 130).

BAGUETTE WITH CHEESE SPREAD

9 oz (250 g) cheddar
2–3 tsp canned green
chile pepper, ½ oz (15 g)
½ bunch chives
1½ oz (40 g) roasted onion
7 tbsp (100 g) crème fraîche
1 wide day-old baguette,
about 12 oz (350 g)
Salt and freshly ground black
pepper

Aluminum foil

Finely grate the cheddar. Drain and chop the green chile pepper. Wash the chives, shake dry, and cut into segments. Mix the chives with the cheddar, green pepper, roasted onion, and crème fraiche. Add salt and pepper.

Cut baguette in half lengthwise and hollow out both halves. Spread the cheese mixture on one half of the baguette, cover it with the other half, and press down. Roll the bread into aluminum foil, place it somewhat higher up on the grill, and grill over high heat for about forty minutes, turning the bread once. Cut the bread into four pieces.

TIP Goes well with the Mexican Skewers (page 30).

80

GRILLED
JAPANESE-STYLE SEITAN

Mix the wasabi, soy sauce, sesame oil, and sesame seeds.

Drain the seitan, pat dry, and cut into four or eight pieces about ⅓ in (1 cm) thick. Grill over high heat for about fifty minutes, turning and brushing with washabi marinade.

Drizzle with the remaining marinade and serve with the drained sushi ginger.

1–2 tbsp wasabi paste

3 tbsp soy sauce

1 tbsp sesame oil

2 tbsp sesame seeds, about ⅓ oz (10 g)

14 oz (400 g) seitan

2 oz (60 g) ginger for sushi

TIP Goes well with the Glass Noodle Salad (page 122).

STUFFED

STUFFED PEPPERS WITH HARISSA COUSCOUS

YIELDS 4 SERVINGS

10 tbsp (100 g) couscous
1 tomato, about 3½ oz (100 g)
2 oz (60 g) sheep cheese
4 parsley sprigs
4 tbsp (60 g) tomato puree
½ tsp Harissa
12 sweet pointed peppers,
about 21 oz (600 g)
2 tbsp olive oil
Salt and freshly ground black pepper

Aluminum foil

1 Bring one cup of salted water to a boil. Add the couscous, bring to boil, and simmer for about five minutes. Wash the tomato, pat dry, and cut into fourths, removing seeds. Cut the tomato flesh and sheep cheese into small cubes. Wash parsley and shake dry. Remove leaves and chop.

2 Mix the tomato puree with the Harissa. Add this mixture to the couscous along with the tomato cubes, sheep cheese, and parsley, mixing everything well. Add salt and pepper.

3 Cut lengthwise down the peppers from stem to end, and remove a wedge from each pepper. Take out the seeds. Wash the peppers and the wedges and pat dry. Chop the wedges into small cubes and add to the couscous. Stuff the peppers with the couscous.

4 Drizzle olive oil over four pieces of aluminum foil. Place about three peppers on each piece of foil. Close the foil pieces and cook over high heat for about ten minutes.

TIP Goes well with the Mint Yogurt (page 112). You can find Harissa in Turkish grocery stores or well-stocked supermarkets.

ANTIPASTO PANINI

½ eggplant, about 5 oz (150 g)

½ zucchini, about 4 oz (120 g)

¼ red bell pepper, about 2 oz (60 g)

¼ yellow bell pepper, about 2 oz (60 g)

1 small red onion

2 garlic bulbs

1 ball of mozzarella, about 4½ oz (125 g)

¼ bunch arugula

10 tbsp (150 ml) Tarragon Oil (page 107)

4 panini loaves

Salt

Aluminum baking pan

1 Wash the eggplant, zucchini, and bell peppers, removing the core from the peppers. Cut the eggplant and zucchini into thin sections and the bell peppers into slivers. Peel the onion and garlic, cutting both into thin rings. Drain the mozzarella and cut into sections. Sort the arugula, wash, drain, and shred.

2 Place the bell peppers, eggplant, and zucchini onto a baking pan. Brush with a small amount of Tarragon Oil and grill over high heat for five minutes. Flip them over and brush again with oil. Add the onion and garlic, and grill for an additional three to five minutes. Meanwhile, cut into the bread loaves and drizzle the remaining Tarragon Oil onto the bread.

3 Lightly salt the grilled vegetables. Stuff the bread with the vegetables, mozzarella, and arugula. Grill the panini over the grate for another five minutes until the cheese begins to melt.

> **TIP** For a piquant substitution, use Taleggio cheese or blue cheese instead of mozzarella.

VEGETARIAN HOT DOG

1 Peel the onions and cucumber and cut them into sections. Wash the lettuce leaves and let them dry. Cut the hot dog buns open.

2 Grill the sausages directly over the grill. Place the onions into a baking pan and grill for about five minutes, rotating and brushing with oil.

3 Grill the buns on the grate for about thirty seconds on each side. Brush the insides with Barbecue Sauce. Fill each with a salad leaf and cucumber slices, and then with sausage and onions on top. Close the buns.

TIP There is a large selection of tofu and seitan sausages available in grocery stores. For this recipe, we really like the smoke-flavored kind.

YIELDS 4 SERVINGS

2 onions
½ cucumber
4 lettuce leaves
4 hot dog buns, about 2 oz each (60 g)
4 smoked tofu sausages,
about 2 oz each (60 g)
Sunflower oil for brushing
4–6 tbsp Barbecue Sauce with
Apricots (page 111)

Aluminum grilling pan

SEITAN BURGER

4 leaves of oak leaf lettuce
½ red bell pepper
½ yellow bell pepper
2 heaping tsp of grainy mustard
7 tbsp (100 g) sour cream
4 ciabatta rolls
7 oz (200 g) seitan
Oil for brushing
7 tbsp (100 g) Onion Relish
(page 115)
Salt and freshly ground black
pepper

1 Wash and drain the lettuce. Wash the bell peppers, remove the core, and chop coarsely. Mix the mustard with the sour cream, salt, and pepper. Cut the ciabatta rolls open. Divide the seitan into four pieces.

2 Grill the bell peppers and seitan over high heat for about five minutes, brushing with oil while grilling. Meanwhile, toast the bread rolls on both sides briefly.

3 Brush the bread with the mustard cream mixture. Place a lettuce leaf on the bottom half of the bread. Cover with seitan, onion relish, and bell peppers. Close the rolls with the remaining bread halves.

TIP Instead of ciabatta rolls, you can make this recipe with flatbreads cut into fourths.

STUFFED CAMEMBERT WITH PUMPERNICKEL

YIELDS 4 SERVINGS

1 Roast the cashews in a small unoiled pan until golden-brown. Chop them together with the cranberries. Wash the parsley, shake dry, remove the leaves, and chop. Crumble the pumpernickel. Mix the cream cheese with the mustard. Mix everything together and add salt and pepper.

2 Cut the Camembert cheeses in half horizontally. Brush four pieces of foil lightly with oil. Place the pumpernickel mixture in four cheese-sized sections on the aluminum foil. Place cheeses over the mixture, rind up, and press down lightly.

3 Close the foil over the cheeses. Grill over high heat for about five minutes until the cheese begins to melt. Serve right away.

TIP Goes well with Onion Relish (page 115).

3½ tbsp (30 g) cashew nuts
3½ tbsp (25 g) dried cranberries
4 parsley sprigs
1 slice of pumpernickel, about 1½ oz
2 tbsp cream cheese
1 tsp Dijon mustard
2 round Camembert cheeses, about 9 oz each (250 g)
Oil for brushing
Salt and freshly ground black pepper

Aluminum foil

93

ONIONS WITH FIG AND GOAT CHEESE TOPPING

2 onions, about 9 oz each (250 g)

2 figs

3–4 thyme sprigs

1–2 tsp Pepper Spice Mix (page 104)

3½ oz (100 g) goat cheese

Oil for brushing

2 tsp wild honey

Salt

Aluminum foil

1 Boil unpeeled onions in salted water for about fifteen minutes. Rinse with cold water and let cool briefly. Peel onions and cut in half.

2 Remove the skins from the figs with a sharp knife. Remove the thyme leaves from the sprigs. Insert some thyme leaves between the onion layers. Salt the onions lightly. Mix the remaining thyme with the fig pulp and spice with one teaspoon of Pepper Spice Mix and salt. Remove the cheese from the rind, crumble it, and add to the mixture.

3 Divide the cheese mixture between the onion halves. Place each onion on a piece of oiled aluminum foil, close the foil into envelopes, and grill for about ten minutes on high heat. Open the foil and drizzle the filling with honey and the remaining Pepper Spice Mix.

TIP If you can, buy the figs when they are very fresh. They do not keep well in the fridge or at room temperature.

STUFFED GRILLED POTATOES

1 Wash the potatoes and boil in water for about thirty-five minutes. Peel the onions and garlic, and chop finely with the drained olives. Wash the oregano, shake dry, remove the leaves, and chop finely.

2 Drain the potatoes and rinse with cold water. Let them stand for a short time. Cut in half lengthwise and hollow out a little with a melon baller. Purée the removed potato with a potato masher. Mix the potato with the prepared ingredients and sour cream. Add salt and pepper.

3 Fill each potato half with the olive-potato mixture. Cover with the other potato half, press together lightly, and wrap each in a piece of foil. Grill the potatoes over high heat for about twenty minutes, rotating.

TIP Goes well with the Wild Herb Salad with Tomatoes (page 125).

4 large potatoes, about
11 oz each (300 g)
1 red onion
1–2 bulbs of garlic
1½ oz (40 g) pitted black olives
4 sprigs of oregano
2 oz (60 g) sour cream
Salt and freshly ground black
pepper

Aluminum foil

97

TOMATOES WITH TABOULEH FILLING

¾ cup (100 g) Bulgur wheat

6 beef tomatoes, about 9 oz each (250 g)

3½ oz (100 g) cucumbers

2 bulbs of garlic

1 bunch of flat-leaf parsley

2–4 sprigs of mint

4 tbsp olive oil

4 tbsp lemon juice

1 oz (30 g) Parmesan cheese

Vegetable oil for brushing

Salt and freshly ground black pepper

Aluminum foil

1 Boil the Bulgur wheat in water for about ten minutes. Wash the tomatoes and pat dry. Cut the tops from the tomatoes and hollow out. Remove the seeds and stems from the tomato tops and cut the rest into small cubes. Wash the cucumbers, peel them if preferred, cut in half lengthwise, and remove the cucumber seeds. Cut them into small cubes. Drain the Bulgur and rinse with cold water, letting dry thoroughly.

2 Wash the garlic and cut into narrow rings. Wash the herbs, shake dry, remove the leaves from the sprigs, and chop the leaves. Mix the olive oil with the lemon juice, salt, and pepper. Mix the Bulgur with the other prepared ingredients and the vinaigrette. Spice to taste.

3 Grate the Parmesan into flakes. Fill the tomatoes with the tabouleh salad and sprinkle the cheese on top. Brush six pieces of foil with oil, place a tomato on each, close the foil over the top, and grill over high heat for about ten minutes.

TIP Goes well with the Baguette with Cheese Spread (recipe on page 80).

SPINACH-STUFFED PORTOBELLO MUSHROOMS

YIELDS 6 SERVINGS

1 Thaw the spinach, press out the moisture, and chop. Mix it with the mascarpone and the Onion Relish. Add salt and pepper.

2 Clean the mushrooms and remove the stems. Mix the oil with salt and pepper and brush the mushrooms. Fill the mushrooms with the spinach mixture, and place each mushroom on a piece of aluminum foil, closing them into packets. Grill over high heat for about ten minutes.

> **TIP** If you like, you can also use fresh spinach. Just wash 3½ oz (200 g) of spinach and blanch it lightly before using the recipe.

7 oz (200 g) frozen spinach

3½ oz (100 g) Mascarpone

2 tbsp Onion Relish (page 115)

4 large portobello mushrooms, about 2 oz each (60 g)

2 tsbp olive oil

Salt and freshly ground black pepper

Aluminum foil

YIELDS 1 OZ (30 G)

1 tbsp black peppercorns
½ tbsp white peppercorns
½ tbsp green peppercorns
½ tbsp pink peppercorns
10 pimiento seeds
1 tsp Fleur de sel
2 rosemary sprigs

Mix peppercorns and pimiento seeds in a mortar and crush them, not too finely.

Add the Fleur de sel and crush with the peppercorns briefly. Wash the rosemary and dry it well. Remove the leaves and chop very finely and add to the spice mix.

TIP If you keep the spice mix in a clean glass container with a secure lid, it will keep for about six months. You could vary the mix by using other types of pepper such as kubeb, Szechuan, or long pepper.

YIELDS 1¼ OZ (35 G)

3 tbsp sesame seeds, about
1 oz (25g)
2 sprigs of lemongrass
2 tsp coarse sea salt

Roast the sesame seeds lightly in an unoiled pan and leave them on a plate to cool. Clean the lemongrass, removing the fibrous outer leaves and finely chopping the inner leaves.

Finely crush half of the sesame seeds in a mortar with the sea salt. Add the remaining sesame and the lemongrass and crush coarsely. The Lemongrass Gomashio will keep for one to two weeks in a closed and clean glass container.

Wash the chili husks, pat dry, cut lengthwise, and remove the seeds. Chop the chili finely. Peel and chop the garlic.

Wash the mint, shake dry, remove the leaves, and chop finely. Mix everything together with the olive oil and salt.

> **TIP** If you prefer a spicier oil, leave the seeds inside the chili husks and chop everything together.

2 husks of red chili
2–3 bulbs of garlic
1 bunch of mint
7 tbsp (100 ml) extra virgin olive oil
1 tsp salt

Wash the tarragon and shake dry. Remove the leaves and chop them finely.
Mix the tarragon with the mustard and the oil, and season with salt and pepper.

> **TIP** Tarragon is especially favored in French cooking. This spiced oil can improve a vinaigrette for a fresh tomato salad and add aroma to grilled goat cheese.

1 bunch of tarragon, about
½ oz (15 g)
1 oz (30 g) grainy mustard
7 tbsp (100 ml) vegetable oil
Salt and freshly ground black pepper

MAPLE SYRUP AND WALNUT MARINADE

2 tbsp shelled walnuts
3½ (100 ml) walnut oil
2 tbsp maple syrup
Juice of ½ orange
Salt and freshly ground
black pepper

Lightly roast the walnuts in an unoiled pan. Let cool and chop. Mix the walnut oil, maple syrup, and orange juice, and season with salt and pepper. Mix in walnuts.

TIP This is a tasty dressing for a mixed green salad or a quick noodle sauce.

FRUIT SALSA

YIELDS 4 SERVINGS

11 oz (300 g) tomatoes
¼ charentais melon, about
9 oz (250 g)
1 shallot
¼ fresh lime
Salt and freshly ground
black pepper

Wash the tomatoes, halve, and remove the seeds. Chop the tomatoes into small cubes. Remove the melon seeds and cut from the rind into similarly sized cubes. Peel and chop the shallot and mix with the tomato and melon chunks.

Wash the lime in hot water, grate the skin, squeeze out a little juice. Season the salsa with salt, pepper, lime rind, and lime juice.

TIP This salsa can be made with any kind of melon. The chanterais has a beautiful color and provides a nice visual touch.

Cut the tomatoes and blanch in boiling water. Drain and rinse with cold water. Remove the tomato skins and cut into coarse chunks. Peel and chop the onion. Wash the apricots, remove the pits, and cut into cubes.

Cook the onion in hot oil until soft. Add the apricots and cook for an additional one to two minutes. Add the tomatoes, sugar, vinegar, tomato paste, and honey. Season with one teaspoon of paprika, two teaspoons of salt, and pepper. Bring to a boil. Cover and cook for fifteen minutes, stirring occasionally.

Simmer the sauce for another ten minutes or so until thick. Season with salt, pepper, additional paprika, and sugar, if desired. Pour the sauce immediately into clean glass containers with tops. Let the sauce cool. It will keep in the closed glass containers for several months.

TIP The barbecue sauce may be used as an excellent substitute for ketchup. If apricots are not in season, you can make the sauce with canned fruit—just add less sugar.

YIELDS 5 GLASSES (EACH ABOUT 1 CUP (200 ML)

2¼ lb (1 kg) plum tomatoes

1 onion

1 lb (500 g) apricots

2 tbsp sunflower oil

About 6 tbsp (70 g) brown sugar

3½ tbsp (50 ml) balsamic vinegar

2 tbsp tomato puree

2 tbsp wild honey

1–2 tsp noble sweet powdered paprika

Salt and freshly ground black pepper

Preserving jars

4 sprigs of mint

11 oz (300 g) creamy

Whole-milk yogurt

1 tsp lemon juice

1–2 pinches of ground cumin

1 pinch of sugar

Salt and freshly ground black

pepper

Wash the mint, shake dry, remove the leaves from the stems, and chop the leaves. Mix the yogurt with the mint and lemon juice. Season with cumin, sugar, salt, and pepper.

TIP For an unusual tzatziki sauce, peel half a cucumber, remove the seeds, grate it roughly, and add to the yogurt.

1 tsp coriander seeds

1–2 husks of red chili

1 bunch of green coriander

9 tbsp (125 g) soft butter

½ fresh lime

Sea salt

Crush the coriander seeds finely in a mortar. Clean the chili and remove seeds. Wash chili and chop it finely. Wash the green coriander, shake dry, pluck the leaves, and chop finely.

Knead the prepared ingredients into the butter. Wash the lime with hot water, grate the peel finely, and squeeze out some juice. Season the butter with salt, lime rind, and a little salt.

TIP The butter can be prepared in advance and kept chilled for one to two days.

APPLE-MANGO CHUTNEY

Peel and pit the mango, cutting fruit into cubes. Peel and core the apple, and cut into cubes. Peel the ginger. Wash the pepper, cut in half lengthwise, and remove the seeds. Finely chop the ginger and pepper.

Mix the prepared ingredients in a pot along with sugar, one teaspoon of salt and the coriander, cinnamon stick, and anise. Add the vinegar and bring to a boil while stirring. Add more vinegar if desired. Pour the hot mixture into clean glass containers and close.

TIP The chutney can be kept in securely closed glass containers in a dark place for six to twelve months. Once opened, keep it refrigerated and use within a few weeks.

YIELDS 1 GLASS (ABOUT 1½ CUPS (350 ML))

1 mango, about 16 oz (450 g)
1 apple, about 5 oz (150 g)
¾ oz (20 g) ginger
1 green chili pepper
8 tbsp (100 g) brown sugar
2 tsp coriander seeds
1 cinnamon stick
1 star anise
5–7 tbsp (70–100 ml) white wine vinegar
Salt

Preserving jars

OLIVE-ALMOND TAPENADE

Drain the olives and coarsely chop with the salted almonds. Peel the garlic and press it into the mixture. Add oil. Season the tapenade with a little salt and pepper.

> **TIP** For this recipe, invest in excellent, high-quality olives.

ONION RELISH

Peel the onions and chop into cubes. Cook the onions in hot oil for five to eight minutes until soft. Add the raisins, mustard seeds, ½ cup of vinegar, and sugar. Bring to a boil. Season with one tablespoon of salt and pepper, cover, and cook for thirty minutes at medium heat, stirring occasionally.

Season the relish with additional vinegar if desired. Let the relish thicken in an uncovered pot for five to ten minutes while stirring. Pour the relish immediately into clean glass containers, cover, and let cool. Refrigerate after opening.

> **TIP** Use high-quality balsamic vinegar with a hint of sweetness.

YIELDS 4 SERVINGS

2 oz (60 g) pitted green olives
2 oz (60 g) pitted black olives
1½ oz (40 g) salted almonds
1–2 cloves of garlic
3 tbsp olive oil
Sea salt and freshly ground black pepper

YIELDS 3 GLASSES (1 CUP (250 ML) EACH)

2¼ lb (1 kg) onions
3 tbsp sunflower oil
¾ (125 g) cup raisins
2 tbsp mustard seeds
½–¾ cup (150–200 ml) balsamic vinegar
½ cup (100 g) brown sugar
Salt and freshly ground black pepper

Clean preserving jars

TO ROUND IT OFF

STRING BEAN AND COUSCOUS SALAD

YIELDS 4-6 SERVINGS

Wash the beans and cut each one in half. Boil for twelve to fifteen minutes in water. Pour the vegetable broth over the couscous in a bowl, let the couscous soak, and cool. Stir with a spoon. Drain the beans, rinse with cold water, and let cool.

Peel and chop the onion. Wash the tomatoes and chop into cubes. Mix both with the couscous and the beans. Season the marinade with lemon juice and orange juice and mix. Cover and let stand for at least two hours.

Wash the arugula, let dry, and shred the leaves. Mix the arugula into the salad just before serving.

9 oz (250 g) string beans
1 cup (200 ml) hot vegetable broth
1 red onion
9 oz (250 g) tomatoes
½ cup (100 ml) maple syrup and Walnut Marinade (page 108)
1–2 tbsp fresh squeezed lemon juice
Orange juice, to taste
1 bunch of arugula
Salt and freshly ground black pepper

TIP Couscous is made out of semolina and presteamed, thus the short soaking time. If the couscous is still too dry after soaking, just add a little more broth.

SPRING SALAD WITH PASSION FRUIT DRESSING

SPRING SALAD WITH
PASSION FRUIT DRESSING

YIELDS 4 SERVINGS

1 bunch white asparagus,
about 18 oz (500 g)
1 bunch of radishes
5 oz (150 g) romaine lettuce
3 passion fruits
1 heaping tsp grainy mustard
1–2 tsp brown sugar
4 tbsp sunflower oil
1 tbsp white wine vinegar, if
needed
Salt and freshly ground black
pepper

Wash and peel the asparagus, cutting off the hard ends. Cut the stalks into thin sections and boil in salted water for four to five minutes, leaving them slightly firm. Drain, rinse, and let cool.

Wash the radishes and cut into fourths. Wash the lettuce, toss until dry, and cut into strips. Mix both with the asparagus.

Halve the passion fruits and scoop out the pulp. Mix with the mustard, sugar, salt, and pepper. Add the oil. Depending on the sourness of the fruit, you may wish to add vinegar. Mix the dressing into the salad.

TIP You can substitute green asparagus in this recipe.
If you do, reduce the cooking time by three minutes.

GLASS NOODLE SALAD

7 oz (200 g) carrots

3½ oz (100 g) sugar snap peas

3 scallions

1 piece of ginger, about ¾ in (2 cm)

1–2 cloves of garlic

2 oz (50 g) salted, roasted peanuts

2–3 tsp sesame oil

5–7 tbsp soy sauce

4 tbsp orange juice

3½ oz (100g) glass noodles

5 coriander stems

1 tbsp rice vinegar

Salt and freshly ground black pepper

Peel the carrots and cut into sticks. Wash the sugar snap peas and leeks, and cut diagonally into thin sections. Peel the ginger and garlic, and chop finely.

Roast the peanuts in an unoiled pan until golden-brown, remove, and chop coarsely. Heat up two teaspoons of sesame oil in a pan and cook the vegetables, ginger, and garlic for about three minutes. Cool the pan down by adding five tablespoons of soy sauce and the orange juice. Season with salt and pepper, and let the mixture cool in a salad bowl.

Soak the glass noodles for ten minutes in cold water. Drain and cover with hot water, soaking for one minute. Drain again and cut to a shorter length with a pair of scissors. Wash the coriander, shake dry, remove the leaves from the stems, and chop coarsely.

Add the noodles, peanuts, and coriander to the vegetables. Season with salt, pepper, vinegar, and, if you like, sesame oil and soy sauce.

TIP This salad goes great with the Grilled Japanese-Style Seitan (page 81).

NOODLE AND LENTIL SALAD

YIELDS 4 SERVINGS

Peel the onion and chop into small cubes. Bring water to a boil and mix in the broth powder. Add the lentils and onion and cook for about twenty minutes. Separately, boil the noodles in salted water for about ten minutes, leaving them slightly firm. Rinse the lentils and the noodles in cold water and let cool.

Mix the mayonnaise, sour cream, apple juice, and chutney. Season with salt and pepper. Mix the noodles and lentils with the salad sauce and let stand for about an hour.

Shortly before serving, wash the apples thoroughly, remove the core, and cut into fourths. Slice the apple quarters into thin sections. Sort the spinach, wash, and toss until dry. Add the spinach and the apples to the noodles and mix. Season to taste.

1 red onion

1 tsp vegetable broth powder

½ cup (100 g) green lentils

¾ oz (200 g) penne pasta

7 tbsp (100 g) mayonnaise

7 tbsp (100 g) sour cream

3 tbsp (50 ml) apple juice

2 tbsp Apple-Mango Chutney (page 113)

2 small sour apples (such as Cox's orange)

3½ oz (100 g) baby spinach

Salt and freshly ground black pepper

> **TIP** This salad may be prepared up to a day in advance. To make it ahead of time, mix the cooked lentils and noodles with the dressing and let them sit in the refrigerator. Then add the apples and spinach and season, if necessary.

123

WILD HERB SALAD WITH TOMATOES

11 oz (300 g) mixed tomatoes

1 oz (30 g) mixed wild herbs (such as dandelion, borage, or nasturtium)

3½ oz (100 g) spring mix salad

3 tbsp dark balsamic vinegar

1 tsp Dijon mustard

1 tbsp liquid honey

4 tbsp olive oil

Salt and freshly ground black pepper

Wash the tomatoes and cut in half or into sections. Wash the herbs and shake dry. Remove the leaves from the stems and coarsely chop the leaves. Wash the spring mix salad and shake dry.

Mix the vinegar with the mustard and honey. Add the oil. Season with salt and pepper. Toss the tomatoes with the spring mix salad and the herbs. Shortly before serving, toss with the vinaigrette.

TIP The salad looks especially inviting when garnished with edible flowers such as daisies or dandelions.

GRILLED ROSEMARY FLATBREAD

GRILLED ROSEMARY FLATBREAD

YIELDS 5 FLATBREADS

2 rosemary sprigs
½ cup (350 g) all-purpose flour
1 packet dry yeast
4 tbsp olive oil
Flour for working
2 tsp Fleur de sel
Fine salt

Wash the rosemary and pat dry. Remove the needles from the stems and chop finely. Mix the flour with the yeast, rosemary, and one teaspoon of fine salt in a bowl. Add one cup (200 ml) of warm water and two tablespoons oil, and knead into a smooth dough. Cover the dough and let stand in a warm place for one to one and a half hours.

Divide the dough into five portions and roll the portions out on a flour-covered surface into flat, oval shapes, about 9 in x 4 in (22 x 10 cm).

Refrigerate the flatbreads prior to grilling, or simply place them immediately over a hot grill. When placing them on the grill, brush one side with olive oil and place that side face down and grill for three to four minutes. Brush the other side with oil and sprinkle over with Fleur de sel. Turn the flatbreads and grill for another three to four minutes.

TIP Cut any leftover flatbread into pieces and use them for a spicy Panzanella salad (Italian bread salad).

126

COLORFUL
SUN ROLLS

Crumble the yeast and mix with sugar in two cups (500 ml) of lukewarm water. Cover and let sit for ten minutes. Mix both types of flour in a bowl with the oil and three teaspoons of salt. Add the yeast mixture and one-third to two-thirds cup (100–150 ml) of lukewarm water to the flour. Knead into a smooth dough. Cover and let sit in a warm place for about ninety minutes.

Drain the tomatoes, let dry, and cut into small pieces. Mix with pine nuts. Coarsely chop pumpkin seeds. Mix dough again with a little flour and divide into three portions. Mix tomatoes and pine nuts into the first dough, the pumpkin seeds into the second, and stir two teaspoons of Lemongrass Gomashio into the third.

Divide each piece of dough into six portions and form into rounded rolls. Lay out parchment paper on baking sheets and set out the rolls into a sun shape while alternating doughs. Cover and let sit for fifteen minutes.

Preheat oven to 420° F (220° C). Brush rolls with cream. Cover Lemongrass Gomashio rolls with remaining Lemongrass Gomashio. Bake for twenty-five minutes until crispy. Let cool.

> **TIP** You can modify the dough as you like—for example, with sunflower seeds, poppy seeds, or chopped herbs.

YIELDS 18 BREAD ROLLS

½ tsp (42 g) yeast

1 tbsp sugar

4 cups (500g) medium to dark rye flour

4 cups (500g) high gluten flour

2 tbsp olive oil

⅓ cup (40 g) sun-dried tomatoes in oil

3½ tsp (25 g) pine nuts

⅓ cup (40 g) pumpkin seeds

Flour for working

4 tsp (10 g) Lemongrass Gomashio (page 104)

2 tbsp cream for brushing

Salt

Parchment paper

129

GRILLED BREAD
WITH CHEESE AND ONIONS

½ cube yeast, about ¼ tsp (21 g)

2 cup (250 g) spelt grain

2 cup (250 g) all-purpose flour

1 tsp salt

½ tsp sugar

3½ oz Emmentaler cheese

1¾ oz (50 g) fried onions

Flour for working

Vegetable oil for brushing

Dissolve the yeast in about one cup (300 ml) of warm water. Mix both types of flour in a bowl along with salt and sugar. Add the yeast water and knead into a smooth dough, adding more water if needed. Cover the dough and set in a warm place for thirty to forty-five minutes.

Finely grate the cheese. Knead the grated cheese and the onions into the dough. Divide the dough into eight portions and form each portion into a ball. Roll the balls out into round flat shapes, about 6 in (16 m) in diameter. Refrigerate the dough before grilling or place immediately over a hot grill. While grilling, brush on both sides with oil and cook for eight to ten minutes over high heat.

TIP The dough may also be used to make campfire bread. To make this bread, divide the dough into about twelve portions. Roll the dough portions into long thin strands. Clean twelve sticks that are long but not too thick, removing bark as needed. Wind the dough around the sticks and cook over the coals (not directly in the fire!) of a campfire or a grill, rotating the sticks constantly.

SUMMER CUCUMBER PUNCH

YIELDS 6 GLASSES, ABOUT 7 OZ (200 ML) EACH

1 cucumber
6 mint sprigs
3 tbsp (40 g) brown sugar
Juice of one lemon
3½ oz Pimm's N° 1
½ L Bitter Lemon soda
¾ pint dry sparkling wine

Wash and peel cucumber. Cut a third of the cucumber into thin slices, cover, and set aside. Cut the rest into coarse chunks. Wash the mint, shake dry, and remove the leaves from the stems. Puree the cucumber chunks with mint and sugar. Add the lemon juice and the Pimm's and let set for at least thirty minutes.

Shortly before serving, add the cucumber slices, the Bitter Lemon, and the chilled sparkling wine. Pour into glasses.

WILD BERRY LEMONADE

YIELDS 6 GLASSES ABOUT 8½ OZ (250 ML) EACH

4 limes
1 husk of vanilla
¾ cup (150 g) sugar
2½ cup (300 g) frozen wild berries
1½ L chilled mineral water

Wash the limes in hot water, dry off, and finely grate the peels. Squeeze the juice of all of the limes. Add water to the juice until the mixture measures one cup. Cut into vanilla husk lengthwise and remove the beans. Add the beans, the husk, the sugar, and the lime rind to the lemon juice and heat to a boil. Simmer uncovered for two to three minutes and let cool.

Meanwhile, thaw the berries. Puree, press through a mesh, and mix with the syrup. Keep cool until ready to serve. Then divide the berry and syrup mixture between glasses and fill with chilled mineral water.

TIP You can also use fresh berries in this lemonade.

INDEX

A

Ajvar

    Eggplant Envelopes with Smoked Tofu 47

Almonds, salted

    Olive-Almond Tapenade 115

Apples

    Apple-Mango Chutney 113

    Fennel and Apple Envelopes with Gorgonzola 56

    Nappa Cabbage Envelopes with Spelt Grain

    Filling 51

    Noodle and Lentil Salad 123

Apple juice

    Noodle and Lentil Salad 123

Apricots

    Barbecue Sauce with Apricots 111

    Halloumi and Apricot Skewers 37

Artichoke Hearts

    Provence Skewers 29

Arugula

    Antipasto Panini 86

    String Bean and Couscous Salad 119

Asparagus, green

    Grilled Asparagus with Goat Cheese 70

Asparagus, white

    Spring Salad with Passion Fruit Dressing 120

Avocado

    Mexican Skewers 31

B

Baguette

    Baguette with Cheese Spread 80

Basil

    Caprese Skewers 28

    Zucchini with Sunflower Seed Pesto 69

Bean Sprouts

    Swiss Chard and Tofu Envelopes 50

Beans, string

    String Bean and Couscous Salad 119

Bitter Lemon

    Summer Cucumber Punch 131

Bourbon vanilla sugar

    Sweet Crêpes with Grilled Peaches 48

Bread Crumbs

    Soy Patties with Olives 66

Brown Sugar

    Apple-Mango Chutney 113

    Barbecue Sauce with Apricots 111

    Grilled Pineapple with Vanilla-Ginger Syrup 74

    Onion Relish 115

    Spring Salad with Passion Fruit Dressing 120

    Summer Cucumber Punch 131

Buffalo mozzarella

    Mozzarella with Persimmon-Tomato Carpaccio 79

Bulgur wheat

    Tomatoes with Tabouleh Filling 98

C

Cabbage, nappa
    Nappa Cabbage Envelopes with Spelt Grain
    Filling

Camembert
    Stuffed Camembert with Pumpernickel 93

Carrots
    Glass Noodle Salad 122

Capers
    Mozzarella with Persimmon-Tomato
    Carpaccio 79

Cashews
    Stuffed Camembert with Pumpernickel 93

Chard, swiss
    Swiss Chard and Tofu Envelopes 50

Charentais melons
    Fruit Salsa 108

Cheese, Cheddar
    Baguette with Cheese Spread 80

Cheese, goat
    Grilled Asparagus with Goat Cheese 70
    Onions with Fig and Goat Cheese Topping 94

Cheese, goat, creamy
    Goat Cheese-Stuffed Grape Leaves 59

Cheese, Sheep
    Flatbread Skewers 33

Stuffed Peppers with Harissa Couscous 85

Cheese, Sheep, creamy
    Stuffed Dates in Phyllo Dough 52

Chili husks, red
    Chili-Mint Oil 107
    Coriander-Chili Butter 112

Chives
    Baguette with Cheese Spread 80

Ciabatta
    Seitan Burger 90

Cinnamon
    Apple-Mango Chutney 113
    Stuffed Dated in Phyllo Dough 52

Coconut milk
    Nappa Cabbage Envelopes with Spelt Grain
    Filling 51

Coriander, green
    Coriander-Chili Butter 112
    Glass Noodle Salad 122

Coriander seeds
    Apple-Mango Chutney 113
    Coriander-Chili Butter 112

Corn
    Gratinated Potatoes 55

Corn cobs
    Corn Cobs with Coriander-Chili Butter

Mexican Skewers 30

Corn, baby
    Marinated Tofu Skewers 24

Couscous
    String Bean and Couscous Salad 119
    Stuffed Peppers with Harissa Couscous 85

Cranberries, dried
    Stuffed Camembert with Pumpernickel 93

Cream Cheese
    Stuffed Dates in Phyllo Dough 52
    Portobello Mushrooms Stuffed with Pine
    Nuts 20

Crème fraîche
    Baguette with Cheese Spread 80
    Sweet Crêpes with Grilled Peaches 48

Cucumber
    Summer Cucumber Punch 131
    Tomatoes with Tabouleh Filling 98
    Vegetarian Hot Dog 89

Cumin, ground
    Goat Cheese-Stuffed Grape Leaves 59
    Mint Yogurt 112

Curry paste, green
    Swiss Chard and Tofu Envelopes 50

Curry powder
    Colorful Soy Sausage Skewers 84

Nappa Cabbage Envelopes with Spelt Grain Filling 51

D

Dates

Stuffed Dates in Phyllo Dough 52

Dijon mustard

Stuffed Camembert with Pumpernickel 93

Wild Herb Salad with Tomatoes 125

E

Eggplant

Antipasto Panini 86

Eggplant Envelopes with Smoked Tofu 47

Provence Skewers 29

Spicy Eggplants 73

Eggs

Soy Patties with Olives 66

Sweet Crêpes with Grilled Peaches 48

Emmentaler

Grilled Bread with Cheese and Onions 130

F

Fennel

Fennel and Apple Envelopes with Gorgonzola 56

Feta cheese (see also Sheep cheese)

Citrus Zucchini-Feta Skewers 27

Figs

Onions with Fig and Goat Cheese Topping 94

Fish sauce

Nappa Cabbage Envelopes with Spelt Grain Filling 51

Flatbread

Flatbread skewers 33

G

Garam Masala

Stuffed Dates in Phyllo Dough 52

Gherkins

Mozarella with Persimmon-Tomato Carpaccio 78

Ginger

Apple-Mango Chutney 113

Glass Noodle Salad 122

Grilled Pineapple with Vanilla-Ginger Syrup 74

Ginger for sushi

Grilled Japanese-Style Seitan 81

Glass noodles

Glass Noodle Salad 122

Gorgonzola cheese

Fennel and Apple Envelopes with Gorgonzola 56

Gouda cheese

Gratinated Potatoes 55

Grape leaves in brine

Goat Cheese-Stuffed Grape Leaves 59

H

Halloumi

Halloumi and Apricot Skewers 37

Halloumi Envelopes with Fruit Salsa 43

Harissa

Stuffed Peppers with Harissa Couscous 43

Herbs de Provence

Provence Skewers 29

Hot dog buns

Vegetarian Hot Dogs 89

K

Ketchup

Colorful Soy Sausage Skewers 34

L

Laurel leaves

Halloumi and Apricot Skewers

Leeks

Nappa Cabbage Envelopes with Spelt Grain Filling 51

Lemon juice

Mangoes with Scallion Vinaigrette 62

Mint Yogurt 112

String Bean and Couscous Salad 119

Summer Cucumber Bowl 131

Tomatoes with Tabouleh Filling 98

Lemongrass

Lemongrass Gomashio 104

Nappa Cabbage Envelopes with Spelt Grain

Filling 51

Lemons

Citrus Zucchini-Feta Skewers 27

Fennel and Apple Envelopes with Gorgonzola 56

Lentils, green

Noodle and Lentil Salad 123

Lettuce, oak leaf

Seitan Burger 90

Limes

Coriander-Chili Butter 112

Fruit Salsa 108

Lime juice

Grilled Pineapple with Vanilla-Ginger Syrup 74

Wild Berry Lemonade 131

M

Makrut lime leaves

Marinated Tofu Skewers 24

Mangoes

Apple-Mango Chutney 113

Mangoes with Scallion Vinaigrette

Maple syrup

Maple Syrup and Walnut Marinade 108

Marsala

Sweet Crêpes with Grilled Peaches 48

Mascarpone

Spinach-Stuffed Portobello Mushrooms 101

Milk

Sweet Crêpes with Grilled Peaches 48

Mozzarella

Antipasto Panini 86

Caprese Skewers 28

Mushrooms, shiitake

Marinated Tofu Skewers 24

Mustard, grainy

Seitan Burger 90

Spring Salad with Passion Fruit Dressing 121

Tarragon Oil 107

Mustard seeds

Onion Relish 115

O

Olives, green

Soy Patties with Olives 86

Stuffed Grilled Potatoes 97

Olive-Almond Tapenade 115

Onions

Onion Relish 115

with Fig and Goat Cheese

Topping 94

Onions, fried

Baguette with Cheese Spread 80

Grilled Bread with Cheese and Onion 130

Onions, white

Colorful Soy Sausage Skewers 34

Orange juice

Colorful Soy Sausage Skewers 34

Glass Noodle Salad 122

Maple Syrup and Walnut Marinade 108

String Bean and Couscous Salad 119

Oregano

Flatbread Skewers 33

Stuffed Grilled Potatoes 97

P

Panini loaves

Antipasto Panini 86

Parsley, flat-leaf

Mozzarella with Persimmon-Tomato Carpaccio 79

Stuffed Camembert with Pumpernickel 93

Stuffed Peppers with Harissa Couscous 85

Tomatoes with Tabouleh Filling 98

Peach

    Sweet Crêpes with Grilled Peaches 48

Pepper, chili, green

    Apple-Mango Chutney 113

Pepper, chili, mild

    Flatbread Skewers 33

Pepper, green bell

    Baguette with Cheese Spread 80

    Barbecue Wrap with Vegetables 44

Pepper, red bell

    Antipasto Panini 86

    Gratinated Potatoes 55

    Mexican Skewers 30

    Seitan Burger 90

Pepper, sweet pointed

    Stuffed Peppers with Harissa Couscous 85

Pepper, yellow bell

    Antipasto Panini 86

    Colorful Soy Sausage Skewers 34

    Seitan Burger 90

Peppercorns, pink

    Citrus Zucchini-Feta Skewers 27

    Pepper Spice Mix 104

Peppermint

    Goat Cheese-Stuffed Grape Leaves 59

Parmesan

Tomatoes with Tabouleh Filling 90

Zucchini with Sunflower Seed Pesto 69

Passion Fruit

    Spring Salad with Passion Fruit Dressing 120

Peanuts, salted, roaste

    Glass Noodle Salad 122

Penne pasta

    Noodle and Lentil Salad 123

Persimmon

    Mozzarella with Persimmon-Tomato

    Carpaccio 78

Phyllo dough

    Stuffed Dates in Phyllo Dough 52

Pimiento seeds

    Pepper Spice Mix 104

Pimientos de Padrón

    Pimiento Skewers 38

Pimm's N° 1

    Summer Cucumber Punch 131

Pineapple

    Grilled Pineapples with Vanilla-Ginger Syrup

Pine Nuts

    Colorful Sun Rolls 129

    Portobello Mushrooms Stuffed with Pine

    Nuts 20

Pistachio, unsalted

Goat Cheese-Stuffed Grape Leaves 59

Grilled Pineapple with Vanilla and Ginger

Syrup 74

Portobello Mushrooms

    Portobello Mushrooms Stuffed with Pine Nuts 20

    Spinach-Stuffed Portobello Mushrooms 101

Potatoes

    Gratinated Potatoes 55

    Potato and Rosemary Skewers 24

    Stuffed Grilled Potatoes 97

Pumpernickel

    Stuffed Camembert with Pumpernickel 93

Pumpkin

    Colorful Sun Rolls 129

R

Radishes

    Spring Salad with Passion Fruit Dressing 120

Raisins

    Onion Relish 115

Romaine lettuce

    Barbecue Wrap with Vegetables 44

    Spring Salad with Passion Fruit Dressing 120

    Kuri Squash with Maple Syrup and Walnut

    Marinade 77

Rosemary

Grilled Rosemary Flatbread 126

Pepper Spice Mix 104

Potato and Rosemary Skewers 23

S

Sage

Portobello Mushrooms Stuffed with Pine
Nuts 20

Scallions

Barbecue Wrap with Vegetables 44

Glass Noodle Salad 122

Gratinated Potatoes 55

Halloumi and Apricot Skewers 37

Mangoes with Scallion Vinaigrette 62

Tomatoes with Tabouleh Filling 98

Seitan

Grilled Japanese-Style Seitan 81

Seitan Burger 90

Sesame oil

Glass Noodle Salad 22

Grilled Japanese-Style Seitan 81

Sesame seeds

Grilled Japanese-Style Seitan 81

Spelt grain

Nappa Cabbage Envelopes with Spelt Grain
Filling 51

Sour Cream

Gratinated Potatoes 55

Noodle and Lentil Salad 123

Seitan Burger 90

Stuffed Grilled Potatoes 97

Soy sauce

Glass Noodle Salad 22

Grilled Japanese-Style Seitan 81

Soy sausage

Soy Patties with Olives

Soy sausage, smoked

Colorful Soy Sausage Skewers 34

Sparkling wine

Summer Cucumber Punch 131

Spinach

Spinach-Stuffed Portobello Mushrooms 101

Spinach, baby

Noodle and Lentil Salad 123

Squash, kuri

Kuri Squash with Maple Syrup and Walnut
Marinade 77

Star anise

Apple-Mango Chutney 113

Sumac

Flatbread Skewers 33

Sugar snap peas

Glass Noodle Salad 122

Sunflower seeds

Zucchini with Sunflower Seed Pesto 69

Sweet potatoes

Barbecue Wrap with Vegetables 44

T

Tarragon

Tarragon Oil 107

Teriyaki marinade

Marinated Tofu Skewers 24

Thyme

Onions with Fig and Goat Cheese Topping 94

Soy Patties with Olives 66

Tofu, firm

Marinated Tofu Skewers 24

Swiss Chard and Tofu Envelopes

Tofu, smoked

Eggplant Envelopes with Smoked Tofu 47

Tofu sausages, smoked

Vegetarian Hot Dog 89

Tomatoes

Flatbread Skewers 33

Fruit Salsa 108

Provence Skewers 29

String Bean and Couscous Salad 119

Stuffed Peppers with Harissa Couscous

Wild Herb Salad with Tomatoes 125

Tomatoes, beef

Mozzarella with Persimmon-Tomato

Carpaccio 78

Tomatoes with Tabouleh Filling 98

Tomatoes, cherry, red

Caprese Skewers 28

Colorful Soy Sausage Skewers 34

Tomatoes, cherry, yellow

Caprese Skewers 28

Wild Herb Salad with Tomatoes 125

Tomatoes, dried

Colorful Sun Rolls 47

Eggplant Envelopes with Smoked Tofu 47

Tomato paste

Barbecue Sauce with Apricots 111

Tomatoes, plum

Barbecue Sauce with Apricots 111

Tomato puree

Stuffed Peppers with Harissa Couscous 85

V

Vanilla husks

Grilled Pineapple with Vanilla-Ginger Syrup 74

Wild Berry Lemonade 131

W

Walnuts, shelled

Maple Syrup and Walnut Marinade 108

Stuffed Dates in Phyllo Dough 52

Walnut oil

Maple Syrup and Walnut Marinade 108

Wasabi paste

Grilled Japanese-Style Seitan 81

Wild berries

Wild Berry Lemonade 131

Wild herbs

Wild Herb Salad with Tomatoes 125

Wild honey

Barbecue Sauce with Apricots 111

Mangoes with Scallion Vinaigrette 62

Onions with Fig and Goat Cheese

Topping 94

Wraps

Barbecue Wrap with Vegetables 44

Y

Yeast

Colorful Sun Rolls 129

Grilled Bread with Cheese and Onions 130

Grilled Rosemary Flatbread 127

Yogurt

Mint Yogurt 112

Z

Zucchini

Antipasto Panini 86

Citrus Zucchini-Feta Skewers 27

Zucchini with Sunflower Seed Pesto 69

THE TEAM

Foto: Kirsten Petersen

Foto: Beata Lange

Foto: Anja Kneller

Maren Jahnke has worked for over eighteen years as a food stylist, recipe developer, and writer for magazines and books, as well as for PR and advertising clients.

Karen Schulz has worked for over fourteen years as a freelance food journalist, recipe developer, and writer for book publishers, magazines, and PR customers for German and European markets. She worked with Maren Jahnke to develop the recipes from this book in their test kitchen in Hamburg.

Wolfgang Kowall has worked as a photographer for over twenty-one years as a freelance food and lifestyle photographer for editorial and advertising clients.

First published in 2012 under the title of VEGETARISCH GRILLEN by Neuer Umschau
Buchverlag GmbH, Moltkestrasse 14, 67433 Neustadt/Weinstrasse, Germany.

Copyright © 2014 by Maren Jahnke and Karen Schulz

Photography copyright © 2014 Wolfgang Kowall

Skyhorse Publishing books may be purchased in bulk at special discounts for sales promotion,
corporate gifts, fund-raising, or educational purposes. Special editions can also be created
to specifications. For details, contact the Special Sales Department, Skyhorse Publishing,
307 West 36th Street, 11th Floor, New York, NY 10018 or info@skyhorsepublishing.com.

Skyhorse® and Skyhorse Publishing® are registered trademarks of Skyhorse Publishing,
Inc. ®, a Delaware corporation.

www.skyhorsepublishing.com

10 9 8 7 6 5 4 3 2 1

Library of Congress Cataloging-in-Publication Data is available on file

Recipes: Maren Jahnke and Karen Schulz, Hamburg
Text: Karen Schulz, Hamburg
Photography: Wolfgang Kowall, Hamburg
Food styling: Maren Jahnke, Hamburg
Requisite: Guenther Meierdierks, Hamburg
Layout and design: Tina Defaux, Neustadt an der Weinstrasse
Cover design: Groothuis, Lohfert, Consorten, Hamburg

Editing: Vanessa Herzog, Neustadt an der Weinstrasse

Printed in China.
ISBN: 978-1-62914-218-0